Michelle Obama

Obama

In Her Own Words

Michelle Obama

In Her Own Words
Young Reader Editon

EDITED BY
Marta Evans
and
Hannah Masters

A B2 BOOK

AGATE

CHICAGO

The Library of Congress has cataloged the earlier edition of this book as follows:

Names: Evans, Marta, editor. | Masters, Hannah, editor.
Title: Michelle Obama in her own words / edited by Marta Evans and Hannah Masters.
Description: Chicago : B2 Books, An Agate Imprint, [2021] | Summary: "A collection of more than 300 quotes from Michelle Obama, author, lawyer, humanitarian, and trailblazing first African American First Lady of the United States of America"-- Provided by publisher.
Identifiers: LCCN 2020051911 (print) | LCCN 2020051912 (ebook) | ISBN 9781572842953 (paperback) | ISBN 9781572848511 (ebook)
Subjects: LCSH: Obama, Michelle, 1964- | Obama, Michelle, 1964---Quotations. | African American women lawyers--Illinois--Chicago--Quotations. | Presidents' spouses--United States--Quotations. | Legislators' spouses--United States--Quotations.
Classification: LCC E909 .M53 2021 (print) | LCC E909 (ebook) | DDC 973.932092--dc23
LC record available at https://lccn.loc.gov/2020051911
LC ebook record available at https://lccn.loc.gov/2020051912

10 9 8 7 6 5 4 3 2 1   22 23 24 25

B2 Books is an imprint of Agate Publishing. Agate books are available in bulk at discount prices. For more information, go to agatepublishing.com.

At fifty-four, I am still in progress, and I hope that I always will be. For me, becoming isn't about arriving somewhere or achieving a certain aim. I see it instead as forward motion, a means of evolving, a way to reach continuously toward a better self. The journey doesn't end.

—MICHELLE OBAMA (2018)

Contents

Introduction 7

Part I: I Had Nothing or I Had Everything: Personal Life

Growing Up in Chicago 12

Education & Career 22

Marriage 28

Parenting 35

Friendships & Community 43

Life Lessons 49

Part II: There Isn't One Right Way to Be an American: Public Life

America: Its Politics & People 57

The White House 64

Role of First Lady 73

Let's Move! & Children's Health 79

Part III: A Better World Is Always Possible: Worldview

Making Change 93

Inequality & Injustice 102

Supporting Women & Girls 108

The Next Generation 113

Milestones 120

Glossary 139

Additional Resources 142

Acknowledgments 144

Introduction

Michelle Obama is optimistic about America—though she would be the first to admit it's not always an easy attitude to maintain. As the first Black First Lady of the United States, she had a unique vantage point from which to witness what America is capable of, both good and bad. With a family history that traces a line from slavery through emancipation and the Great Migration to the height of power in the U.S., her story reflects tragic American injustices alongside the American hope of overcoming them.

In 1964 on Chicago's South Side, Michelle LaVaughn Robinson was born to Marian Robinson, a secretary, and Fraser Robinson III, a city water plant worker who put in long hours despite having multiple sclerosis. The family was working-class and lived in a small apartment where Michelle and her older brother Craig shared a room split by a wooden divider. It was a childhood full of warmth and freedom, with long days spent playing outside and a tradition of family meals. Marian and Fraser encouraged the children to explore and ask questions. Michelle recalls demanding why she had to eat eggs for breakfast, which she didn't like. When her parents said it was because she needed protein, she lobbied, strategically, for peanut butter and jelly sandwiches as a replacement—and won.

Her parents were frank about what it would take for a Black girl like Michelle to succeed—that along with her talent and intelligence, she would need exceptional dedication to reach her goals. The Robinsons set their expectations high, both for her schoolwork and her responsibilities to her family and community. Michelle, who took her parents' work ethic as a model, was reading by age four and was enrolled in a gifted program by sixth grade. She went on to attend Chicago's first public magnet high school, where she was a member of the National Honor Society and served as student council treasurer.

Her hard work paid off. Despite the doubts of at least one college counselor, who told Michelle, "I'm not sure you're Princeton material," she graduated as the salutatorian (typically the second-highest ranked student) and was admitted to Princeton with a work-study scholarship. Though she excelled in her college classes, she often felt alienated at the majority-white school and sought refuge in her connections to the small group of other Black students. She carried these experiences with her to Harvard Law School, where she worked to increase diversity on campus.

After Harvard, Michelle returned to Chicago and took a position at the well-respected law firm Sidley Austin. Soon, she was assigned to mentor a summer associate named Barack Obama. Barack showed immediate interest in her, but she initially declined, wary of dating a coworker. When she agreed to a date, the relationship quickly grew serious. Three years later, they were married.

Michelle, who had begun to question her satisfaction with corporate law, left the firm for public service roles in city government and nonprofits. These changes were due partly to Barack's encouragement to take risks and pursue her interests. But it was also the loss of her father, who died in 1991 at age 55, that caused her to reconsider her priorities. Her father had taught her the value of keeping your word and showing up for other people. She wanted to honor his memory by keeping these values at the center of her life and work.

Barack, in his own search for meaningful work, had set

his sights on politics. Michelle was less than thrilled. She had long held doubts about politicians, whom she felt acted mainly out of self-interest. But she trusted Barack and didn't want to stand in his way. Cautiously, she supported him through his successful campaign for Illinois State Senate in 1996.

The demands of Barack's political schedule became more difficult after the birth of their first daughter, Malia, in 1998. Three years after their second daughter, Sasha, was born in 2001, Barack eyed a U.S. Senate seat. Michelle made him promise that if he lost the race, he would get out of politics altogether. But he didn't lose. Michelle juggled her own career with caring for the children in Chicago while Barack commuted to Washington. As his popularity increased following a speech at the 2004 Democratic National Convention, Michelle was swayed by the idea that the truths he stood for could be put into action on the national political stage. Even so, she agreed to his presidential campaign without really believing he would win.

As she scaled back her career to accompany Barack on the campaign trail, Michelle's own fame grew. Though many voters responded to her humor and honesty, she was intensely watched by the press and political opponents. Hostility has always been present in politics, but race played a large role in the attacks made against the Obamas, which often subtly—and sometimes openly—painted Michelle as the stereotype of the "angry Black woman." Nevertheless, with the support of a broad and energetic group of voters, the Obamas were elected to the White House.

Michelle Obama carefully considered what kind of First Lady she would be. Despite the pressures of the public eye, she made it her mission to continue to present her authentic self. Aspects that made her unusual among first ladies—her race, her working-class upbringing, her notable career path, her education (she was the third First Lady in history with a graduate degree)—allowed her to speak in a personal way to women of color, working mothers, girls who dreamed big, families who struggled to make ends meet, and so many others. Her two young daughters were always her priority in the White House and being "mom-in-chief" also informed her public projects. The Let's Move! initiative, which aimed to provide children with access to and education about nutritious food, arose from the memory of her own difficulties ensuring Malia and Sasha had healthy meals while she worked full-time. Similarly, through Let Girls Learn, she connected her hopes for her daughters' education to educational justice work for girls all over the world.

During her time in the White House, Michelle Obama's approval ratings often outstripped her husband's. As a private citizen, her popularity has remained high. In her memoir, *Becoming*, she shared her successes and struggles in more detail, hoping her story would be an inspiration. Despite being repeatedly nudged toward a political career, her focus remains on serving the public outside of elected office by lending her name to get out the vote campaigns and starting new initiatives to fight for the causes close to her heart. Michelle carries no illusions about the difficulty of making change, especially for those whom society leaves most vulnerable. But she argues that it is precisely for this reason that optimism is a commitment worth making—that our faith in a better future is what helps us achieve it.

Part I

PERSONAL LIFE

I Had Nothing or I Had Everything

Growing Up in Chicago

CHICAGO IS THE city that taught me what it means to give back.

—**Instagram, May 31, 2019**

EVEN THOUGH OUR family was crammed into a tiny apartment, one of the greatest gifts [my mom] gave me was the freedom to explore and develop into my own person.

—**Instagram, May 10, 2019**

MY FATHER GAVE us absolutely everything. The laughs and lessons, the hugs, the heartache from losing him—they're all still there with me, every minute.

—**Instagram, April 14, 2019**

YEAH, I WENT to Princeton and Harvard, but the lens through which I see the world is the lens that I grew up with. I am the product of a working-class upbringing. I grew up on the South Side of Chicago in a working-class community.

—**"Michelle Obama on Elitism,"** *The New York Times*, **April 15, 2008**

[GRANDMA] WAS PERHAPS my first example of a professional woman, showing me that being graceful and being in command weren't mutually exclusive.

—**Instagram, September 8, 2019**

EDITORIAL NOTE: The grandmother Obama is referring to is her father's mother, LaVaughn Robinson. She was the manager of a bookstore that sold bibles on Chicago's South Side.

EVERY PARENT'S FIRST job is to keep their kids safe. But sometimes that instinct can get out of hand.... No one understood that better than my mother, Marian Robinson. She gave my brother, Craig, and me the freedom to roam—not just in our neighborhood, but within our own minds and **burgeoning** moral codes.

—*The National*, Amtrak, August/September 2019

> BURGEONING (adj.): growing or developing

WHEN I WAS still in elementary school, my dad bought my brother a pair of boxing gloves. But when he came home from the store, he was carrying not one, but two pairs of gloves. He wasn't going to teach his son to punch without making sure his daughter could throw a left hook, too.

—*Vogue*, July 29, 2019

FROM AN EARLY age, [my mom] saw that I had a flame inside me, and she never **tempered** it. She made sure that I could keep it lit.

—Instagram, May 12, 2019

TEMPERED (verb): lessened or made less powerful

WE CONSTANTLY FELT the struggle to balance our family responsibilities and the schoolwork, the activities, and the goals that we had for ourselves. And through it all, my parents fully expected us to do both—to achieve our dreams, and be there for our family.

—Let Girls Learn in London, June 16, 2015

OUR VOICES HAD real value in our house. There's some people who raise kids and they use the **philosophy** 'kids are to be seen and not heard,' and it was just the opposite for us.

—"Meet the Author: Michelle Obama," Virgin, December 11, 2018

PHILOSOPHY (noun): an idea about how people should live or behave

WHEN I THINK of [Euclid Avenue, Chicago], when I think of our childhood, I think of music. Music was the backdrop of everything. We didn't do anything without music, and that's because our father was a big jazz lover and had a huge jazz album collection that he cherished.

—**"Growing Up Robinson with Craig and Michelle,"** ***The Michelle Obama Podcast,*** **August 19, 2020**

WHAT I SAW in our father was that nothing replaces getting on the phone and calling somebody, showing up for somebody.

—**"Growing Up Robinson with Craig and Michelle,"** ***The Michelle Obama Podcast,*** **August 19, 2020**

THERE WERE VICTORY gardens everywhere. Families that were poor—folks that came from large families, like my parents, where there were six, seven kids each—you relied heavily on those gardens to incorporate vegetables. And that was a tradition.

—*CookingLight*, **February 6, 2015**

EDITORIAL NOTE: Victory gardens were common in the United States during World War II. These neighborhood gardens provided fruits and vegetables for people in the U.S. at a time when food was sometimes hard to find. The gardens also allowed people to feel they were supporting the war effort and part of the community.

MY DAD WAS a shift worker, so there were some dinner times when he was at work, but whenever he was there we would sit around the table with the plastic tablecloth, and that's when we would catch up and we'd talk about what we were eating, talk about what was going on in the day.

—*CookingLight*, **February 6, 2015**

> **EDITORIAL NOTE:** Shift workers sometimes work differ-
> ent shifts, or work periods, on different days. For instance, a
> company that organizes work into shifts might have one group of
> employees work from 5:00am to 1:00pm and then have another
> group of employees work from 1:00pm to 9:00pm, and might
> have workers rotate between the day shift and the evening shift.

I ADORED MY brother. I have been 'Craig
Robinson's little sister' for most of my life. And I
could have an attitude about it, but I am a fan too.

**—"Michelle Obama says her brother is still their
mother's favorite,"** *Good Morning America,* **November
13, 2018**

UNLIKE MY MOM, we didn't learn how to cook.
That wasn't something my mother stressed for
me. We came from the generation where my
mom wanted me to go to college and law school,
and she always said, 'You'll learn how to cook,'
but that's not something she pressed.

—*CookingLight,* **February 6, 2015**

My DAD, HE'S our rock. To grow up with a dad with a disability, who never complained, went to work every day, didn't miss a day of work. Never remember Dad being sick or talking about being sick. When you grow up with that kind of drive and those values, we just never wanted to disappoint him.

—**"Michelle Obama says her brother is still their mother's favorite,"** *Good Morning America*, **November 13, 2018**

EDITORIAL NOTE: Obama's father had multiple sclerosis (MS), a disease that affects the body's nervous system and can interfere with communication within the brain or between the brain and the rest of the body.

I AM AND always will be a Robinson. That means a lot of things, but maybe most of all, it means I show my love by sharing stories. We are a soulful, **boisterous** bunch of South Siders, always at our best when crowded around a kitchen table, cracking jokes and catching each other up on the ups and downs of our lives.

—*The National*, **Amtrak, August/September 2019**

> **BOISTEROUS** (adj.): noisy and full of energy

I GREW UP with a disabled dad in a too-small house with not much money in a starting-to-fail neighborhood, and I also grew up surrounded by love and music in a diverse city in a country where an education can take you far. I had nothing or I had everything. It depends on which way you want to tell it.

—*Becoming*, p. 416, November 2018

Education &

Career

THE ABILITY TO read, write, and analyze. The confidence to stand up and demand justice and equality. The qualifications and connections to get your foot in that door and take your seat at the table. All of that starts with education.

—Let Girls Learn Event Celebrating International Women's Day, March 8, 2016

IT REMINDED ME of my dad, you know? Working class folks that are doing jobs that aren't that fun, but it pays the bills. So it showed me the respect I needed to have for the folks who work every day, and it sent me straight to college.

—on her first job at a book-bindery, "First Lady Michelle Obama Talks Her Firsts," *The Tonight Show*, February 21, 2014

MY WHOLE IDENTITY was bound up in checking those boxes, winning every award I could, and I was good at it too. By the time I got to my high school graudation, I was at the top of my class, member of the National Honor Society, student class treasurer, and my college dream had come true—I was heading to Princeton that fall.

—**commencement address at Martin Luther King, Jr. Magnet High School, May 18, 2013**

EDITORIAL NOTE: The National Honor Society recognizes high school students who have earned a high grade point average, performed community service, served as leaders in their schools, and demonstrated character traits such as honesty and respect for others.

I HAVE FOUND that at Princeton no matter how liberal and open-minded some of my White professors and classmates try to be toward me, I sometimes feel like a visitor on campus; as if I really don't belong.

—**"Michelle Obama's Career Timeout,"** *The Washington Post*, **May 11, 2007**

I TRIED TO recreate a community of comfort for myself and I did that by pretty much staying very close to the black community that was there. It was a place of comfort for me in this **bastion** I call it. I was a poppy seed in a sea of whiteness.

—on finding community at Princeton, "Michelle Obama Shares Her Chicago Lessons," WBEZ 91.5, November 13, 2018

BASTION (noun): a protected place

I KNOW HOW it feels to be overlooked. To be underestimated. To have someone only half-listen to your ideas at a meeting.

—Let Girls Learn Event Celebrating International Women's Day, March 8, 2016

LOSING MY DAD **exacerbated** my sense that there was no time to sit around and ponder how my life should go. . . . If I died, I didn't want people remembering me for the stacks of legal briefs I'd written or the corporate trademarks I'd helped defend. I felt certain that I had something more to offer the world. It was time to make a move.

—*Becoming*, **p. 146, November 2018**

EXACERBATED (verb): made more extreme

PUBLIC ALLIES WAS all about promise—finding it, nurturing it, and putting it to use. It was a **mandate** to seek out young people whose best qualities might otherwise be overlooked and to give them a chance to do something meaningful. To me, the job felt almost like destiny.

—**on working for Public Allies,** *Becoming*, **p. 176, November 2018**

> **EDITORIAL NOTE:** Public Allies is a national organization that helps people enter careers in public service and nonprofit work.

> **MANDATE** (noun): order or command

I DIDN'T GROW up with a lot of money. I never even imagined being the First Lady of the United States. But because I had an education, when the time came to do this, I was ready.

—**"First Lady's Dance Moves Woo Indian Crowds,"** *The New York Times*, **November 8, 2010**

Marriage

IF MY UPS and downs, our ups and downs in our marriage can help young couples sort of realize that good marriages take work … It's unfair to the institution of marriage, and it's unfair for young people who are trying to build something, to project this perfection that doesn't exist.

—"The Obamas' Marriage," *The New York Times*, **October 26, 2009**

MARRIAGE IS A choice you make every day. It can be hard work, but when two people commit to seeing that work through, the rewards are as sweet as they come.

—**Twitter, May 21, 2020**

EDITORIAL NOTE: The Obamas were married on October 3, 1992. At the time of this quote, they had been married for almost 28 years.

THIS IS ONE of the things I love about Barack. . . .
He grew up with a single mom, his grandmother
was the true head of household, he married me,
he's got Malia and Sasha, who do not mince their
words, and he has sustained himself through a
life of strong women.

—**"Michelle Obama on Keeping Marriage, Politics
Separate," ABC News, October 8, 2012**

EDITORIAL NOTE: When someone is described as not mincing their words, that means they say what they mean in a direct and honest way, even if what is being said might be difficult for the listener to hear.

AND MEETING BARACK Obama and falling in love
with him and having somebody in your life that
you cared about that influenced you and encouraged you to take some risks helped me begin to
start my swerve and to leave the law and start
going into public service and working for the
government.

—**"Michelle Obama Shares Her Chicago Lessons,"
WBEZ 91.5, November 13, 2018**

BUT WE DIDN'T always live in the White House. And for many years before coming to Washington, I was a working mother, doing my best to juggle the demands of my job with the needs of my family, with a husband who has crazy ideas.

—**"Michelle Obama's remarks at Workplace Flexibility Conference,"** *The Washington Post*, **March 31, 2010**

MARRIAGE IS HARD, and raising a family together is a hard thing. It takes a toll. But if you're with the person, if you know why you're with them, if you understand that there is a friendship and a foundation there, it may feel like it goes away during those hard times, but it's something that we always come back to.

—**"Oprah's 2020 Vision Tour Visionaries: Michelle Obama Interview," February 12, 2020**

[BARACK] GREW UP without his mother in his life for most of his years, and he knew his mother loved him dearly, right? I always thought love was up close. Love is the dinner table, love is consistency, it is presence. So I had to share my **vulnerability** and also learn to love differently.

—*O, The Oprah Magazine*, **December 2018**

> **VULNERABILITY** (noun): a quality of emotional openness that often reveals a person's fears or weaknesses

I AM LIKE a lit match. It's like, poof! And he wants to **rationalize** everything. So he had to learn how to give me, like, a couple minutes—or an hour—before he should even come in the room when he's made me mad. And he has to understand that he can't convince me out of my anger.

—*O, The Oprah Magazine*, **December 2018**

> **RATIONALIZE** (verb): explain with reason or logic

IT'S JUST ME and [Barack] and Bo and Sunny at dinner, and they don't talk—the dogs don't—so we're looking at each other.

—**"Oprah's 2020 Vision Tour Visionaries: Michelle Obama Interview," February 12, 2020**

EDITORIAL NOTE: When Barack Obama was running for president, he promised his children that whether he won or lost the family would get a dog when the election was over. Bo joined the first family in 2009, and Sunny became part of the Obama household in 2013. Bo and Sunny are both Portuguese Water Dogs.

[BARACK] DOESN'T UNDERSTAND fashion. He's always asking, 'Is that new? I haven't seen that before.' It's like: 'Why don't you mind your own business? Solve world hunger. Get out of my closet.'

—**"Wrapped in Their Identities," *The New York Times*, December 24, 2009**

WE ARE HAPPY people, but why wouldn't we be? We have our health. We have each other. We have a sense of purpose.

—**"Oprah and Michelle Obama: Your Life in Focus,"** ***Oprah's SuperSoul Conversations*, February 12, 2020**

[THE PRESIDENCY] HAS definitely brought us closer. It wasn't until we moved to the White House that we were together seven days a week, that we could have dinner together, that he had time to coach the girls' teams, and go to all the events.

—**"The Final Interview With The Obamas (Full Interview)," PeopleTV, December 20, 2016**

I CAN LOOK at him [Barack] and I still recognize my husband. He's still the man that I fell in love with, who I value and I respect and I trust. He's been an amazing father through so much. He has shown up well in the world. He has been who he promised he would be to me.

—**"Oprah's 2020 Vision Tour Visionaries: Michelle Obama Interview," February 12, 2020**

Parenting

KIDS WILL MODEL what they see at home, and the values that are promoted at home, so whether they have a lot or a little, they still know what their parents believe and what they expect.

—**"Meet the Author: Michelle Obama," Virgin, December 11, 2018**

BARACK AND I were both raised by families who didn't have much in the way of money or material possessions, but who had given us something far more valuable: their unconditional love. Their **unflinching** sacrifice. And a chance to go places they had never imagined for themselves.

—**Democratic National Convention, September 4, 2012**

UNFLINCHING (adj.): refusing to turn away from an unpleasant situation

FIRST OF ALL, you gotta have a mate that shares your values.... Parenting is a verb. It is an active, engaging thing.

> —**"Oprah's 2020 Vision Tour Visionaries: Michelle Obama Interview,"** February 12, 2020

I'M GOING TO try to take them to school every morning—as much as I can.... I like to be a presence in my kids' school. I want to know the teacher; I want to know the other parents.

> —**"Michelle Obama to Grace Cover of Vogue Magazine,"** *The Washington Post*, February 10, 2009

EVERY OTHER MONTH [since] I've had children I've struggled with the notion of 'Am I being a good parent? Can I stay home? Should I stay home? How do I balance it all?' I have gone back and forth every year about whether I should work.

> —**"Michelle Obama's Career Timeout,"** *The Washington Post*, May 11, 2007

I AM IN awe of my children for the way they have managed this whole thing with poise and grace. There's a **resilience** that they've had to develop.

—*Conan O'Brien Needs A Friend,* **March 17, 2019**

RESILIENCE (noun): the ability to find happiness or success after facing challenges or hardships

MOTHERHOOD HAS ALSO taught me that my job is not to bulldoze a path for them in an effort to eliminate all possible **adversity**. But instead, I need to be a safe and consistent place for them to land when they inevitably fail; and to show them, again and again, how to get up on their own.

—*Vogue,* **July 29, 2019**

ADVERSITY (noun): a difficult or challenging situation

WHAT I TELL my kids is, 'All I can do is give you the information. All I can do is model those choices. And all I can do is help you understand the consequences of your choices, and then I've gotta be with you as you make those choices and give you some feedback.'

—**"First Lady: Nation's Health 'Starts With Our Kids',"** ***Talk of the Nation*, June 12, 2012**

[ADOLESCENCE IS] THE period of our lives when we're finding our own voices and for the first time making independent decisions that help us figure out the person we'll become. That's why those years can be confusing and **exhilarating** and **devastating**, all at once.

—***Good Housekeeping*, December 3, 2018**

EXHILARATING (adj.): causing strong feelings of happiness and excitement

DEVASTATING (adj.): causing significant emotional or physical harm

---

WHAT I AM saying is that parenting takes up a lot of emotional space, and, you know, my husband was busy being president, so I don't think he understood how much time and energy . . . I put a lot of time and energy into parenting these girls in the White House, because we were trying to make their lives normal.

—**"Oprah's 2020 Vision Tour Visionaries: Michelle Obama Interview," February 12, 2020**

EDITORIAL NOTE: When Barack Obama was first elected president, Sasha and Malia were seven and ten years old, respectively. At the end of Obama's two terms in office, his daughters were fifteen and eighteen years old.

MANY WOMEN GET up before dawn to get a workout in or to **savor** a few minutes of alone time before the kids wake up. And I want to give all those women a big hug and let them know that there are millions of women like me who've been through it—and we've got your backs.

—*Good Housekeeping*, **December 3, 2018**

SAVOR (verb): fully enjoy or appreciate

THERE ARE MANY different approaches that
we try to use normalizing [Sasha and Malia's]
experience. Setting the same set of expectations
for our children that our parents had for us. You
know, contributing around the house. Not taking
your advantages for granted.

—"Meet the Author: Michelle Obama," Virgin,
December 11, 2018

HAVING [SASHA AND Malia] in schools where
some kind of **mandatory** community service
was a part of the curriculum has always been
important to me.

—"Meet the Author: Michelle Obama," Virgin,
December 11, 2018

MANDATORY (adj.): required

MALIA, FOR HER gap year, spent three months in the Amazon camping. I didn't want her to do that, but I thought what an important lesson in **resilience** for her, just physically, to know that she could endure something that hard and be away from home in a different country, learning a different language. So I had to have the courage to let her do that, even though I desperately wanted her to just be close to home.

—**"Meet the Author: Michelle Obama," Virgin, December 11, 2018**

RESILIENCE (noun): the ability to find happiness or success after facing challenges or hardships

EDITORIAL NOTE: A "gap year" is a break that some students take between high school and college. Often students who take a gap year use that time to work, travel, or participate in nontraditional learning experiences.

Friendships &

Community

I'll QUIT ON myself faster than I'll quit on my friends.

> —**"What Your Mother Never Told You About Health with Dr. Sharon Malone,"** *The Michelle Obama Podcast*, **August 12, 2020**

I'M A PEOPLE person, so being with good friends is always a **salve** for me. In the White House, one of the best things I could do for myself was to invite a friend over just to talk.

> —*Good Housekeeping*, **December 3, 2018**

SALVE (noun): a remedy that is soothing

I THINK WE underestimate the desire for people to feel a connection to each other. We take that for granted.

> —**"Oprah's 2020 Vision Tour Visionaries: Michelle Obama Interview," February 12, 2020**

WE **GRAVITATE** TO one another when we see the best and the worst in ourselves, because it makes us feel human.

—"Oprah's 2020 Vision Tour Visionaries: Michelle Obama Interview," February 12, 2020

GRAVITATE (verb): to be drawn to a person, place, or idea

EVEN IN HARD times, our stories help cement our values and strengthen our connections. Sharing them shows us the way forward.

—Instagram, April 27, 2020

WHEN WE PULL ourselves out of the lowest emotional depths and we channel our frustrations into studying and organizing and banding together, then we can build ourselves and our communities up. We can take on those deep-rooted problems and together . . . together we can overcome anything that stands in our way.

—commencement address at Tuskegee University, May 12, 2015

WHY DID I leave corporate law and go into community service? The truth is, it was selfish. I was happier. When I left that firm and started working in the city and getting out into the broader community of Chicago and seeing the interconnectedness of these neighborhoods, but being alive in the dirt and the grit of helping people, I never looked back.

—**"President Barack Obama,"** *The Michelle Obama Podcast*, **July 29, 2020**

EDITORIAL NOTE: Corporate law covers all of the legal issues a corporation may face. People who work in corporate law focus on rules and regulations related to how a business is created, conducted, and managed.

WE CAN'T SHOW up for the world if we don't take care of ourselves first.

—**Instagram, August 10, 2020**

WHENEVER I HAVE moments of fear or anxiety, I try to find ways to connect with others. I might call someone who I know is struggling and just let them know that I'm thinking of them. That simple act of reaching out lifts my spirits, too.

—*O, The Oprah Magazine,* **April 15, 2020**

THE PROBLEM IS, we don't know each other, we don't let each other in. And I said in [*Becoming*], it is hard to hate up close. It is easier to hate when you are hating a person through a filter.

—*The Late Show with Stephen Colbert,* **December 1, 2018**

EDITORIAL NOTE: *Becoming* is Michelle Obama's memoir in which she talks about her personal life, professional career and activism, and experience living and working in the White House.

IN AN UNCERTAIN world, time-tested values like honesty and **integrity**, **empathy** and compassion, that's the only real currency in life. Treating people right will never, ever fail you.

—"Dear Class of 2020" Commencement Address, June 7, 2020

INTEGRITY (noun): the quality of having strong moral values
EMPATHY (noun): the ability to understand and be sensitive to the feelings or thoughts of another person

Life

Lessons

IF I COULD tell my younger self one thing, it would be to slow down and take a breath—you've got this.

—**Instagram, February 12, 2020**

I HAVE LEARNED that as long as I hold fast to my beliefs and values and follow my own moral compass, then the only expectations I need to live up to are my own.

—**commencement address at Tuskegee University, May 12, 2015**

EDITORIAL NOTE: A "moral compass" refers to a person's values and judgments by which they guide their lives and their choices. When someone makes a decision based on their feelings of what is right, they are using their moral compass.

AS A CHILD, my first doll was Malibu Barbie. That was the standard for perfection. That was what the world told me to **aspire** to. But then I discovered Maya Angelou, and her words lifted me right out of my own little head.

—**Maya Angelou's Eulogy, June 7, 2014**

> **ASPIRE** (verb): to want to reach a certain life goal or achievement

> **EDITORIAL NOTE:** Maya Angelou was a writer, poet, and activist who is best known for her autobiographical works with themes of social, economic, and racial oppression. Angelou was also a civil rights activist, participating in the civil rights movement for equal rights for Black Americans in the 1950s and 1960s.

WOMEN OF COLOR know how to get things done for our families, our communities, and our country. When we use our voices, people listen. When we lead, people follow. And when we do it together, there's no telling what we can accomplish.

—**Instagram, September 11, 2018**

WHEN I ENCOUNTERED doubters, when people told me I wasn't going to cut it, I didn't let that stop me—in fact, I did the opposite. I used that negativity to fuel me, to keep me going.

—**Bell Multicultural High School, November 12, 2013**

PART ONE *Life Lessons*

MICHELLE OBAMA IN HER OWN WORDS 51

WHAT WE OFTEN see as a weakness or a failure is often a strength—or a turning point to something better.

—Instagram, December 30, 2019

AND I THOUGHT to myself, 'If I died today, is this where I wanna be?' And it wasn't just one thing. It was a few things that made me step back and say, 'Alright, put down the boxes and the checks and now you have to do the hard work of thinking about who you want to become.'

**—*"Becoming,* Part 1," *All Things Considered,*
November 9, 2018**

BECOMING WHO WE are is an ongoing process, and thank God—because where's the fun in waking up one day and deciding there's nowhere left to go?

—*Vogue,* July 29, 2019

ACT WITH BOTH your mind but also your heart.

**—commencement address at Tuskegee University,
May 12, 2015**

AT FIFTY-FOUR, I am still in progress, and I
hope that I always will be. For me, becoming isn't
about arriving somewhere or achieving a certain
aim. I see it instead as forward motion, a means
of evolving, a way to reach continuously toward a
better self. The journey doesn't end.

—*Becoming*, **p. 419, November 2018**

I WANTED TO live my life by the principle that to
whom much is given, much is expected.

**—commencement address at Martin Luther King, Jr.
Magnet High School, May 18, 2013**

EDITORIAL NOTE: The phrase "to whom much is given, much
is expected" refers to a phrase in the New Testament of the Bible.
As a guiding principle, this phrase references the idea that people who are given opportunities, privileges, or responsibilities in
life are expected to use what they are given to help others.

JOB TITLES AND fancy awards come and go, but
our lives are really made up of the little moments
and connections in between.

—*O, The Oprah Magazine*, **April 15, 2020**

ONE OF THE lessons that I grew up with was to always stay true to yourself and never let what somebody else says distract you from your goals. And so when I hear about negative and false attacks, I really don't invest any energy in them, because I know who I am.

—*Marie Claire*, **October 22, 2008**

MY JOURNEY HAS taught me that if we stay open—if we share what's important to us and listen carefully to what others share about their own lives—we find our strength, and we find our community.

—**Instagram, May 4, 2020**

I CONTINUE, TOO, to keep myself connected to a force that's larger and more **potent** than any one election, or leader, or news story—and that's optimism. For me, this is a form of faith, an **antidote** to fear.

—*Becoming*, **p.420 November 2018**

> **POTENT** (adj.): very strong or effective
> **ANTIDOTE** (noun): a remedy that soothes or reduces harm

IT'S EASY TO lead by fear. It's easy to be **divisive**. It's easy to make people feel afraid. That's the easy thing, and it's also the short term thing. And for me, what I learned from my husband, what I learned in eight years at the White House is that this life, this world, our responsibility in it, is so much bigger than us.

—**"Oprah's 2020 Vision Tour Visionaries: Michelle Obama Interview," February 12, 2020**

> **DIVISIVE** (adj.): prompting disagreement and often leading to the formation of opposing points of view or groups

YOUR STORY IS what you have, what you will always have. It is something to own.

—*Becoming*, **p. xi, November 2018**

Part II

PUBLIC LIFE

**There Isn't One Right Way to
Be an American**

America: Its Politics & People

WE ARE HERE because we believe in some simple truths, that no child's future should be limited because of the neighborhood they are born in. We believe that if you get sick in America, you should be able to see a doctor. We believe that if you work hard, you should make a decent wage and have a secure retirement.

—**"Party Stars' Last Push to Democratic Faithful,"** *The New York Times*, **November 1, 2010**

EDITORIAL NOTE: The Obama presidency was marked by progressive social policies, such as access to equal education, affordable healthcare, a living wage, and retirement benefits. The Affordable Care Act, which enacted a policy of providing affordable health insurance coverage for all Americans, was passed in March 2010.

BEING PRESIDENT DOESN'T change who you are, it reveals who you are.

—**Democratic National Convention, August 17, 2020**

CHILDREN BORN IN the last eight years will only know an African-American man being president of the United States. That changes the bar for all of our children, regardless of their race, their sexual orientation, their gender. It expands the scope of opportunity in their minds. And that's where change happens.

—*Parade*, **August 15, 2013**

YOU'RE JUDGED IN your community because you're not Black enough, and then you get out in the world, and you're too Black. And it's a careful tightwalk that we all walk as underrepresented people in the world, because people aren't used to your voice.

—**"Becoming, Part 2,"** *All Things Considered*,
November 9, 2018

IF EVER I'M feeling sorry for myself, or I'm feeling down, spending some time talking with the men and women who are the spouses of our service members that makes you understand that there is no problem that you can't handle, because they do it all with grace, and with dignity. They don't complain.

—**"Michelle Obama & Dr. Jill Biden On Their Husbands' Bromance & More,"** *Entertainment Weekly*, **December 15, 2016**

IF WE DON'T know who people are inside, if we don't trust their instincts and understand where they're coming from, then we can't follow them, which is why we've tried to be so open and clear about who we are and how we think.

—**"Wife Touts Obama's 'Moral Compass',"** *The Washington Post*, **May 8, 2007**

THE ABILITY TO vote freely, fairly—and safely—is bigger than any single issue, party, or candidate.

—**Twitter, May 21, 2020**

I KNOW THAT I am dealing with some form of low-grade depression, not just because of the quarantine but because of the racial strife and just seeing [the Trump] administration, watching the hypocrisy of it day in and day out is **dispiriting**.

—**"Protests and the Pandemic with Michele Norris,"** ***The Michelle Obama Podcast,*** **August 5, 2020**

EDITORIAL NOTE: The murder of George Floyd by Minnesota police officer Derek Chauvin was one of many incidents of police brutality towards Black Americans during the summer of 2020; a summer that was also marked by the continuation of the COVID-19 pandemic and the isolation recommended to minimize its spread. Throughout that summer, protestors clashed with police in major cities across the country, calling for justice and greater protections for Black Americans and sparking global social justice movements.

DISPIRITING (adj.): prompting a lack of hope or excitement

IT DOESN'T MATTER what you or I think at this point, it's up to the voters now to figure out what kind of moral leadership do we demand in the White House? Regardless of party, regardless of race, regardless of gender, regardless of where you are, what do we want our president to look like? How do we want them to act? And if we vote for one set of behaviors, then that's obviously what we want, until we vote differently.

—*The Late Show with Stephen Colbert,* **December 1, 2018**

SOMETIMES TRUTH **TRANSCENDS** party.

—Twitter, June 18, 2018

> TRANSCENDS (verb): overcomes limits or boundaries

WE GROW UP with messages that tell us that there's only one way to be American—that if our skin is dark or our hips are wide, if we don't experience love in a particular way, if we speak another language or come from another country, then we don't belong. That is, until someone dares to start telling that story differently.

—*Becoming*, **p. 415, November 2018**

THESE DAYS, IT can be hard to feel grounded or hopeful—but the connections I've made with people across America and around the world remind me that **empathy** can truly be a lifeline.

—**Twitter, April 27, 2020**

EMPATHY (noun): the ability to understand and be sensitive to the feelings or thoughts of another person

The White House

IF YOU CAN'T run your own house, you can't run the White House.

—**"Michelle Obama: Did She or Didn't She?,"** *The New York Times*, **August 21, 2007**

IT'S IMPORTANT FOR young people, in particular our kids, kids of all backgrounds, of every race, and every **socioeconomic background**, to feel like they have a place in the Nation's house. And to do that, you have to do things that make them comfortable as well. And if it's hip-hop dancing, well let's do it, you know? If it's a sleepover on the south lawn with the Girl Scouts, then let's do it.... Let's breathe some life into this house.

—**"The Final Interview With The Obamas (Full Interview),"** **PeopleTV, December 20, 2016**

SOCIOECONOMIC BACKGROUND (noun): related to social and economic factors, such as a person or family's financial situation, education, and access to resources

I'LL ALWAYS BE grateful for the opportunity that living in the White House afforded us, but it probably won't come as a surprise to anyone that sometimes it was a real challenge to keep up with the pace. We'd be launching an **initiative**, or crisscrossing the country for campaign events, or visiting a community that was hurting from a tornado or a senseless shooting—sometimes all in a two- or three-day span.

—*Good Housekeeping*, **December 3, 2018**

INITIATIVE (noun): a plan or policy that is designed to solve a particular issue

---

I DON'T LOSE sleep over it, because the realities are, you know, as a Black man, Barack can get shot going to the gas station. You can't make decisions based on fear and the possibility of what might happen. We just weren't raised that way.

—**on if she worries the Presidency makes Barack a target for violence, "A Political Phenomenon," *60 Minutes*, December 25, 2008**

THE PRESSURE WAS on everyone. We couldn't afford to make a mistake, we couldn't afford to look **cavalier**. We had to watch our language. And we also knew that everything we said . . . we thought about how it would be viewed by children, not just our children, but all of our children. We knew that we were the moral compass.

—*The Late Show with Stephen Colbert*, **December 1, 2018**

CAVALIER (adj.): acting in a dismissive or uncaring manner

WHEN YOU'RE NOT engaged in the day-to-day struggles that everybody feels, you slowly start losing touch. And I think it's important for the people in the White House to have a finger on the pulse.

—*Vogue*, **November 11, 2016**

EDITORIAL NOTE: To have a "finger on the pulse" means to have a strong sense of current issues and sentiments, especially in a social and political context. This includes public opinion on policies and movements. During the Obama presidency, relevant issues included affordable healthcare, climate change, social justice, and LGBTQ equality.

WE WANTED TO change things up here in the White House a little bit. We wanted to open the doors really wide to a bunch of different folks who usually don't get access to this place. We also wanted to highlight all different kinds of American art—all the art forms: paintings, music, culture—especially art forms that had never been seen in these walls.

—*"Hamilton* at the White House" workshop, March 14, 2016

EDITORIAL NOTE: *Hamilton* is a Broadway musical that utilizes genres of hip-hop, rap, rhythm and blues, and jazz music to tell the story of founder Alexander Hamilton. The show spotlights cultural, ethnic, and racial diversity in its casting, dance, and musical numbers, much of which had not been typically featured at the White House by previous administrations.

THE TRIPS THAT we did take as a family are ones that we'll remember for the rest of our lives. They're not normal family vacations and those experiences have definitely brought us together in ways that we wouldn't have if we weren't here.

—"The Final Interview With The Obamas (Full Interview)," PeopleTV, December 20, 2016

EDITORIAL NOTE: During their time in the White House, the Obama family took international trips to Cuba, Brazil, Argentina, Ghana, Russia, France, and the United Kingdom. They also took multiple domestic trips, visiting various national parks and Barack Obama's home state of Hawaii.

THIS IS THE first time in a long time in our marriage that we've lived seven days a week in the same household with the same schedule, with the same set of **rituals**. That's been more of a relief for me than I would have ever imagined.

—"The Obamas' Marriage," *The New York Times*, October 26, 2009

RITUALS (noun): actions that are repeated multiple times in the same way

I THINK, FOR Barack, having somebody who's like the big brother ... in this journey, somebody that he respects and admires. It's the best decision that Barack has made as President of the United States, picking Joe and the Bidens as our partners in this journey. That's real.

—**"Michelle Obama & Dr. Jill Biden On Their Husbands' Bromance & More,"** *Entertainment Weekly*, **December 15, 2016**

EDITORIAL NOTE: Joe Biden served as vice president to Barack Obama from 2008 to 2016 before becoming the 46th president of the United States in 2020. Biden has a long history in public office, serving as a United States senator from Delaware from 1973 to 2008. While in the Senate, Biden focused on foreign relations and criminal justice, matters on which he advised the president during his role as vice president.

YES, THE JOB carries its stresses, for sure.... When you feel that burden, you really have to fall back on the normalcy and the love of your family. I think probably some of the best moments for Barack were when he could come up on that elevator, come to the second floor, sit down at the dinner table and have no one care about anything he does. At all. I mean, literally. Just talked over, talked around. 'Oh, by the way, Dad. Oh yeah, what did you do today?'

> —**"The Final Interview With The Obamas (Full Interview)," PeopleTV, December 20, 2016**

REFLECTING, I FIND, is very important. The truth is that for the last decade, there was no time to even really think about what just happened to us.

> —***The Jimmy Kimmel Show*, November 16, 2018**

THE FREEDOM THAT we'll get in exchange for the privileges and the luxuries, you know.... Seven and a half years, that's enough **luxuriating**. I can make my own grilled cheese sandwich. I can make a mean grilled cheese sandwich.

—**"Carpool Karaoke,"** *The Late Late Show with James Corden*, **July 21, 2016**

LUXURIATING (verb): indulging in an activity or experience that is enjoyable

---

WE ARE FINDING each other again. We have dinners alone and chunks of time where it's just us—what we were when we started this thing: no kids, no publicity, no nothing. Just us and our dreams.

—*People*, **November 26, 2018**

Role of First Lady

THERE IS NO handbook for incoming First Ladies of the United States. . . . It's a strange kind of sidecar to the presidency, a seat that by the time I came to it had already been occupied by more than forty-three different women, each of whom had done it in her own way.

—*Becoming*, p. 283, November 2018

I WAS HUMBLED and excited to be First Lady, but not for one second did I think I'd be sliding into some glamorous, easy role. Nobody who has the words 'first' and 'Black' attached to them ever would.

—*Becoming*, p. 284, November 2018

MY VIEW ON this stuff is I'm just trying to be myself, trying to be as authentic as I can be. I can't pretend to be somebody else.

—"Michelle Obama's Career Timeout," *The Washington Post*, May 11, 2007

WHEN YOU'RE FIRST Lady, America shows itself to you in its extremes.

—*Becoming*, p. x, November 2018

ELEANOR ROOSEVELT IS one of my idols. She is probably one of the greatest first ladies that has ever lived, with her active engagement in this country and being able to shift norms in ways that are important.

—*CookingLight*, February 6, 2015

EDITORIAL NOTE: Eleanor Roosevelt was first lady during her husband Franklin D. Roosevelt's four terms in office from 1933 to 1945. As a humanitarian activist, Eleanor is best known for her public service, charity, and volunteerism in various areas of social reform, such as racial and gender equality and protections for working people and children. Eleanor's contributions as first lady also included her acting in lieu of her husband and making public appearances and attending conferences on his behalf, as the president was ill during much of his time in office.

I MAINTAINED A code for myself, though, when it came to speaking publicly about anything or anyone in the political sphere: I said only what I absolutely believed and what I absolutely felt.

—*Becoming*, p. 407, November 2018

HOW BARACK AND I **comported** ourselves in the face of instability mattered. We understood that we represented the nation and were obligated to step forward and be present when there was tragedy, or hardship, or confusion. Part of our role, as we understood it, was to model reason, compassion, and consistency.

—*Becoming*, p. 343, November 2018

COMPORTED (verb): behaved in a way that is considered appropriate to a certain situation or role

THERE HAD BEEN so many times in my life when I'd found myself the only woman of color—or even the only woman, period—sitting at a conference table or attending a board meeting or mingling at one VIP gathering or another. If I was the first at some of these things, I wanted to make sure that in the end I wasn't the only—that others were coming up behind me.

—Becoming, **p. 355, November 2018**

I NEEDED TO demonstrate to the nation that I can do the work. I work hard and I work smart, and let me just show you. And in the end I have to count on the fact that what I produce will define me. And so that's what it means to go high. In the end, don't seek revenge, don't **harbor** resentment. Just do the work.

—Conan O'Brien Needs A Friend, **March 17, 2019**

EDITORIAL NOTE: During the 2016 presidential election, Michelle Obama spoke the phrase "when they go low, we go high" in support of Democratic presidential nominee Hillary Clinton, which then became a famous and commonly quoted phrase. To "go low" refers creating divisiveness with negative insults. To "go high" means to rise above negativity, refusing to respond with something equally "low."

HARBOR (verb): to hold on to certain feelings for a long period of time

OF COURSE I am proud of my country. Nowhere but in America could my story be possible.

—**"Michelle Obama Shows Her Warmer Side on 'The View'," *The New York Times*, June 19, 2008**

I TAKE THE words that I say to children very seriously. When I am with a young person, I want them to hear me see them. It's important for them to know that this person, who's so famous and has this platform, thinks that they are beautiful and smart and kind and good. And that has meaning.

—**"Oprah's 2020 Vision Tour Visionaries: Michelle Obama Interview," February 12, 2020**

Let's Move! & Children's Health

RARELY IN THE history of this country have we encountered a problem of such **magnitude** and consequence that is so **eminently** solvable. So instead of just talking about this issue, or worrying and wringing our hands about it, we decided to get moving.

—*American Grown: The Story of the White House Kitchen Garden and Gardens Across America*, p. 178, **May 2012**

MAGNITUDE (noun): large in importance and size
EMINENTLY (adv.): highly

THIS ISN'T ABOUT inches and pounds or how our kids look. It's about how our kids feel and how they feel about themselves.

—**"First Lady Michelle Obama: 'Let's move' and work on childhood obesity problem,"** *The Washington Post*, **February 10, 2010**

I HAVE YET to meet a single parent who doesn't understand the threat of obesity to their health and to their children's health. And they're looking for solutions.

—Let's Move! Food Marketing, September 18, 2013

EDITORIAL NOTE: During the Obama presidency and prior to the "Let's Move!" initiative, the childhood obesity rate was 17%, and 12.7 million children were considered obese. Despite the initiative, the childhood obesity rate stayed at 16.9% from 2008 to 2012. From 2010 to 2012, during the "Let's Move!" initiative, the obesity rate for children ages two to five decreased by 3.7%, but the rate for children twelve to nineteen increased by 2.1%.

FROM THE BEGINNING, I knew I wanted children to play a major role in the creation and growth of our garden. I particularly wanted to include local kids who had never dreamed of visiting the White House despite living in the same city.

—American Grown: The Story of the White House Kitchen Garden and Gardens Across America, p. 54, May 2012

I ALSO KNEW that I wanted this new White House garden to be a 'learning garden,' a place where people could have a hands-on experience of working the soil and children who have never seen a plant sprout could put down seeds and seedlings that would take root. And I wanted them to come back for the harvest, to be able to see and taste the fruits (and vegetables) of their labors.

—*American Grown: The Story of the White House Kitchen Garden and Gardens Across America*, p. 10, **May 2012**

WE EVENTUALLY SETTLED on a spot at the back edge of the South Lawn that could easily be seen from outside the White House gate. That was important to me because I wanted this to be the people's garden, just as the White House is the 'people's house.' I wanted people who were just walking by to be able to share in what we were doing and growing.

—*American Grown: The Story of the White House Kitchen Garden and Gardens Across America*, p. 31, **May 2012**

> **EDITORIAL NOTE:** For security purposes, the White House grounds are not open to the public, except for guided tours. A gate surrounds the White House lawns and gardens.

IN FACT, EQUALITY is a key part of the message of planting day. We are all down in the dirt. Anyone present can help dig. There is no **hierarchy**, no boss, and no winner. It is almost impossible to mess up. We make it clear that gardening isn't about perfection.

—*American Grown: The Story of the White House Kitchen Garden and Gardens Across America*, **p. 54**
May 2012

> **HIERARCHY** (noun): a classification system where people are placed into a ranking order, with one group at the top and one at the bottom

WITHOUT ANYONE EXPECTING it, our garden has become a community garden, connecting people from all different backgrounds, ages, and walks of life. We all share in its care and in its success; and here in this garden, each of us, in our own way, has been able to put down roots.

> —*American Grown: The Story of the White House Kitchen Garden and Gardens Across America*, p. 86–87 May 2012

EDITORIAL NOTE: The phrase "walks of life" refers to diverse backgrounds, recognizing the fact that everyone's life experiences are unique.

I've HULA-HOOPED AND done push-ups on the White House lawn. I've jumped Double Dutch and run through an obstacle course of cardboard boxes carrying water jugs. I've potato-sack raced with comedian Jimmy Fallon. I've even danced 'the Dougie' to Beyoncé with a bunch of middle schoolers. But there's a method to my madness. We know that as parents, we are our kids' first and best role models, and I want kids to see that there are all kinds of ways to be active.

—American Grown: The Story of the White House Kitchen Garden and Gardens Across America, **p. 199, May 2012**

EDITORIAL NOTE: "Double Dutch" is a style of jumping rope in which two ropes are turned in opposite directions at the same time.

WHILE OUR GOAL was ambitious, the idea behind Let's Move! was very simple: that all of us—parents and teachers; doctors and coaches; business, faith, and community leaders; and others—have a role to play in helping our kids lead healthier lives.

—American Grown: The Story of the White House Kitchen Garden and Gardens Across America, p. 178, **May 2012**

THOSE FIRST SEEDS we planted in our garden helped start a conversation that grew into a nationwide movement as people across this country united to address the challenge of childhood obesity. And together, with determination and creativity, we have begun building the foundation for a healthier generation and a healthier nation.

—American Grown: The Story of the White House Kitchen Garden and Gardens Across America, p. 165, **May 2012**

THIS ISN'T ABOUT trying to turn the clock back to when we were kids or preparing five-course meals from scratch every night. No one has time for that. And it's not about being 100 percent perfect, 100 percent of the time. Lord knows I'm not. There's a place for cookies and ice cream, burgers and fries—that's part of the fun of childhood.

—**"First Lady Michelle Obama: 'Let's move' and work on childhood obesity problem,"** *The Washington Post*, **February 10, 2010**

A LOT OF kids don't understand that food is fuel in a very fundamental way. And sometimes they don't listen to grown-ups, and they don't listen to the First Lady. But many of them will listen to you [fellow kids] because you're living proof of that reality.

—**Kids' State Dinner, July 10, 2015**

FROM THE TIMES our kids are still in diapers, we as parents are already fighting an uphill battle to get them interested in the foods that will actually **nourish** them and help them grow.

—Let's Move! Food Marketing, September 18, 2013

NOURISH (verb): feed in a sustainable and satisfying way

As BOTH A mother and a First Lady, I was alarmed by reports of skyrocketing childhood obesity rates and the **dire** consequences for our children's health. And I hoped this garden would help begin a conversation about this issue—a conversation about the food we eat, the lives we lead, and how all of that affects our children.

—*American Grown: The Story of the White House Kitchen Garden and Gardens Across America*, p. 9, May 2012

DIRE (adj.): very serious in nature

AT THE WHITE House Kitchen Garden, we want
kids to witness the entire journey of their food,
from soil to table. So at our very first fall harvest,
we invited them into the White House kitchen,
where they helped cook a meal of grilled chicken,
salad, brown rice, peas, and honey cupcakes. We
didn't know whether the kids would like the vegetables, but they devoured the salad and asked
for more.

—American Grown: The Story of the White House
Kitchen Garden and Gardens Across America, **p. 125,**
May 2012

WE ALSO KNOW that we need to attack this problem from every angle, because we can serve kids the healthiest school lunches imaginable, but if there's no supermarket in their community, and they don't have **nutritious** food at home, then they still won't have a healthy diet. We can build shiny new supermarkets on every block, but if parents don't have the information they need, they'll still struggle to make healthy choices for their kids. And if kids aren't active, then no matter how well we feed them, they still won't be leading healthy lives.

—American Grown: The Story of the White House Kitchen Garden and Gardens Across America, p. 178–180, May 2012

NUTRITIOUS (adj.): possessing the types of vitamins and other elements that people need to stay healthy

IT'S A SOCIAL justice issue. Every child in this country, every person in this country, should have access to good food.

—"**First Lady Michelle Obama: 'Let's move' and work on childhood obesity problem,**" *The Washington Post*, **February 10, 2010**

> **EDITORIAL NOTE:** "Social justice" refers to concepts of equality and freedom for all people, particularly for those that are historically oppressed and lack equal social and economic opportunities. As a movement, social justice involves activism and education in order to promote and obtain equal access to resources and privileges for people of all races, ethnicities, genders, sexualities, and religions.

Part III

WORLDVIEW

**A Better World Is Always
Possible**

Making

Change

A FAIRER, MORE just, and more loving world is always possible.

—Twitter, June 26, 2020

WE WANT OUR children—and all children in this nation—to know that the only limit to the height of your achievements is the reach of your dreams and your willingness to work for them.

—Democratic National Convention, August 25, 2008

ONE THING I know is that it's up to us to be there for each other—especially those who often feel overlooked—because when someone shows genuine interest in your growth and development, it can make all the difference in the world.

—Instagram, March 6, 2019

THINGS GET BETTER when regular folks take action to make change happen from the bottom up. Every major historical moment in our time, it has been made by folks who said, 'Enough,' and they banded together to move this country forward—and now is one of those times.

—**"Michelle Obama's family tree has roots in a Carolina slave plantation,"** ***The Chicago Tribune,*** **December 1, 2008**

EDITORIAL NOTE: President Obama was elected to his first term in office on November 4, 2008, making him the first Black man elected to the office of the U.S. presidency. This quote also refers to the overall policies of the Obama presidential campaign, which focused on social and economic change.

THIS IS HOW you can finish the work that the generations before you started. By staying open and hopeful, even through tough times. Even through discomfort and pain.

—**Twitter, June 7, 2020**

I BELIEVE THAT each of us—no matter what our age or background or walk of life—each of us has something to contribute to the life of this nation.

—Democratic National Convention, August 25, 2008

MAKE A DECISION to use your privilege and your voice for the things that really matter. . . . Share that voice with the rest of the world. For those of you that feel invisible, please know that your story matters. Your ideas matter. Your experiences matter. Your vision for what the world can and should be matters.

—"Dear Class of 2020" Commencement Address, June 7, 2020

EDITORIAL NOTE: "Privilege" refers to the opportunities, status, and power someone is or isn't given in society based on their race, class, gender, sexual orientation, and religion. People of marginalized identities have historically been afforded less privilege, and to "use your privilege" means to use the opportunities and power you have to advocate for people who don't have equal opportunities.

ANGER IS A powerful force. It can be a useful force, but left on its own, it will only **corrode** and destroy and sow chaos on the inside and out. But when anger is focused, when it's **channeled** into something more, that is the stuff that changes history.

—**"Dear Class of 2020" Commencement Address, June 7, 2020**

CORRODE (verb): slowly destroy
CHANNELED (verb): directed energy in a specific way

WE CANNOT ALLOW our hurt and our frustration to turn us against each other, to cancel somebody else's point of view if we don't agree with every last bit of their approach. That kind of thinking only divides us and distracts us from our higher calling. It is the gum in the wheel of progress.

—**"Dear Class of 2020" Commencement Address, June 7, 2020**

EDITORIAL NOTE: To "cancel" someone refers to an action commonly found on social media where people, often in a large group, call out something controversial or offensive someone has said with the intention of getting the person to address their past comments. Some people refer to this action as "canceling" someone's career or following. However, many celebrities or public figures who say they have been "canceled" still retain their platforms and presence.

WHEN SOMETHING DOESN'T go your way, you've just got to adjust. You've got to dig deep and work like crazy. And that's when you'll find out what you're really made of.

—**commencement address at Martin Luther King, Jr. Magnet High School, May 18, 2013**

YOUR GREATEST ACHEIVEMENTS will never come easily, and they will never be achieved alone.

—**graduation banquet speech at West Point, May 23, 2011**

THROUGH SERVICE, WE can heal ourselves.

—**commencement address at Virginia Tech, May 14, 2012**

CAUSE I DON'T want you to think that when you have a problem you're broken. I think that, that's the message. If I'm perfect, then when you're not, which is **inevitable**, you think you're failing. And it's like no, you're just living life.

—**"Best of: Becoming Michelle Obama,"** *2 Dope Queens,* **March 12, 2019**

> INEVITABLE (adj.): unavoidable

NO MATTER WHAT path you choose, I want you to make sure it's you choosing it and not someone else.

—**commencement address at Tuskegee University, May 12, 2015**

REMEMBER TO ALWAYS stay open to new experiences and never let the doubters get in the way.

—**Instagram, December 19, 2018**

HISTORY IS MADE by the people who show up for the fight, even when they know they might not be fully recognized for their contributions.

—*Harper's Bazaar*, June 22, 2020

FOR SO MANY people, TV and movies may be the only way they understand people who aren't like them. It becomes important for the world to see different images of each other, so that we can develop **empathy** and understanding.

—*Variety*, August 23, 2016

EMPATHY (noun): the ability to understand and be sensitive to the feelings or thoughts of another person

IT'S NOT WHO'S in the White House. It's not who is the First Lady. You can give a lift, but once you give people that information, and help them understand that they have the power to make the change, then change actually happens.

—*Variety*, August 23, 2016

TOO OFTEN, WE focus on what I call our 'stats.' What school did you go to? What's your occupation? But the truth is, to really get to know people, we have to go deep into those stories. I felt that if I wanted people to get to know me, I had to share everything.... And that's really the way I live my life.

—**"Meet the Author: Michelle Obama," Virgin, December 11, 2018**

I AM MAKING my mark in hopes that my grandchildren will experience something better than I did, just as my parents laid down markers so that my life would be better than theirs. We don't fix things in a lifetime.

—**"Becoming, Part 2,"** *All Things Considered*, **November 9, 2018**

EDITORIAL NOTE: Michelle Obama's notes in her book *Becoming* that her parents worked hard to provide for her and her brother. Her mother worked as a secretary and her father worked at a water filtration plant.

Inequality

&

Injustice

EVEN THOUGH THE story has never been tidy, and Black folks have had to march and fight for every inch of our freedom, our story is nonetheless one of progress.

—**Instagram, June 19, 2020**

EDITORIAL NOTE: During the civil rights movement in the 1950s and 1960s, civil rights leaders often organized marches as a way to advocate for equal rights for Black Americans. The March on Washington in 1963, where Martin Luther King Jr. gave his "I Have a Dream" speech, is cited as one of the leading factors in the passing of the Civil Rights Act of 1964, which banned discrimination based on a person's race, religon, sex, or nation of origin. The marches from Selma to Montgomery in protest of voter suppression also contributed to the passing of the Voting Rights Act of 1965, which bans discrimination based on a voter's race.

IF WE WANT to keep making progress on issues like racial justice, we've got to be willing to start hard conversations––especially with the people we love.

—**Instagram, July 27, 2020**

THERE WILL ALWAYS be folks who make assumptions about you based on **superficial** things like where you're from or what you're wearing or how you look. There will always be folks who judge you based on just one thing that you say or do, folks who define you based on one isolated incident.

—commencement address at Virginia Tech, May 14, 2012

SUPERFICIAL (adj.): on a surface level

I REMEMBERED THEM all, every person who'd ever waved me forward, doing his or her best to **inoculate** me against the slights and indignities I was certain to encounter in the places I was headed—all those environments built primarily for and by people who were neither Black nor female.

—*Becoming*, p. 355, November 2018

> INOCULATE (verb): protect against harm

WAKING UP TO yet another story of a Black man or a Black person somehow being dehumanized or hurt or killed or falsely accused of something, it is exhausting. And it has led to a weight that I haven't felt in my life in a while.

—**"Protests and the Pandemic with Michele Norris,"** ***The Michelle Obama Podcast*, August 5, 2020**

WHEN IT COMES to all those tidy stories of hard work and self-determination that we like to tell ourselves about America, well, the reality is a lot more complicated than that. Because for too many people in this country, no matter how hard they work, there are structural barriers working against them that just make the road longer and rockier.

—**"Dear Class of 2020" Commencement Address, June 7, 2020**

THAT IS THE story of this country.... The story of generations of people who felt the lash of **bondage**, the shame of servitude, the sting of segregation, but who kept on striving and hoping and doing what needed to be done, so that today, I wake up every morning in a house that was built by slaves. And I watch my daughters, two beautiful, intelligent, Black young women, playing with their dogs on the White House lawn.

—Democratic National Convention, July 25, 2016

BONDAGE (noun): enslavement

GOING HIGH DOES not mean putting on a smile and saying nice things when confronted by viciousness and cruelty. Going high means taking the harder path, means scraping and clawing our way to the mountaintop. Going high means standing fierce against hatred.

—Democratic National Convention, August 17, 2020

IF WE EVER hope to move past [racism], it can't just be on people of color to deal with it. It's up to all of us—Black, white, everyone—no matter how well-meaning we think we might be, to do the honest, uncomfortable work of rooting it out.

—Instagram, May 29, 2020

WHAT TRULY MAKES our country great is its diversity. I've seen that beauty in so many ways over the years. Whether we are born here or seek refuge here, there's a place for us all. We must remember it's not my America or your America. It's our America.

—Twitter, June 19, 2019

Supporting Women & Girls

WE KNOW THAT when we give girls a chance
to learn, they'll seize it. And when they do, our
whole world benefits.

—**Instagram, September 5, 2019**

WHEN I GET up and work out, I'm working out
just as much for my girls as I am for me, because I
want them to see a mother who loves them dearly, who invests in them, but who also invests in
herself. It's just as much about letting them know
as young women that it is okay to put yourself a
little higher on your priority list.

—*Prevention Magazine*, **January 31, 2012**

RAISING STRONG GIRLS isn't just about what we
do as women—it's about the example the men in
their lives set, too.

—**Twitter, June 16, 2019**

FOR A GIRL to have strong men in her life, like I had, a father who loved me, a brother who adored me and cared for me, made me stronger.

—**"Michelle Obama says her brother is still their mother's favorite,"** *Good Morning America,* **November 13, 2018**

THERE ARE FEW things that inspire me like seeing the potential of adolescent girls around the world.

—**Twitter, October 11, 2018**

THERE ARE MORE than 62 million girls around the world who are not in school—girls whose families don't think they're worthy of an education, or they can't afford it.... Girls like Malala Yousafzai who are assaulted, kidnapped, or killed just for trying to learn. And this isn't just a **devastating** loss for these girls, it's a **devastating** loss for all of us who are missing out on their promise.

—**Let Girls Learn in London, June 16, 2015**

> **DEVASTATING** (adj.): causing significant emotional or physical harm

> **EDITORIAL NOTE:** Malala Yousafzai is a Pakistani activist who advocates for equal education for girls across the globe. She survived an attempt on her life by the Taliban when she was fifteen and went on to become the youngest Nobel Peace Prize laureate in 2014.

IF THESE TEN women can endure death threats and horrifying violence and years behind bars to stand up for what they believe in, then surely our young people can find a way to stand up for what they believe in.

—on the ten honorees at the International Women of Courage Award Ceremony, March 8, 2012

WHEN WE VIEW [girls'] voices as equal, when we truly listen to them and appreciate what they say, they will feel more **empowered** to share themselves with the rest of the world, too.

—Instagram, May 10, 2019

EMPOWERED (adj.): feeling confident and supported

I BELIEVE EVERY girl on the planet deserves the same kind of opportunities that I've had—a chance to fulfill her potential and pursue her dreams.

—Instagram, September 5, 2019

The Next

Generation

WHEN WE TALK about the potential of our young people, we often think about it as some far-off promise, years or decades away. But the truth is they have so much to offer us right now.

—Instagram, August 1, 2019

WE MUST CONFRONT wrong and outdated ideas and assumptions that only certain young people deserve to be educated, that girls aren't as capable as boys, that some young people are less worthy of opportunities because of their religion or disability or ethnicity or **socioeconomic class**. Because we have seen time and again that potential can be found in some of the most unlikely places.

—"The age of youth: Traveling abroad, First Lady Michelle Obama makes kids Topic 1," *The Washington Post*, April 15, 2010

SOCIOECONOMIC CLASS (noun): standing in a society related to social and economic factors, such as a person or family's financial situation, education, and access to resources

NEVER EVER BE embarassed by those struggles. You should never view your challenges as a disadvantage. Instead, it's important for you to understand that your experience facing and overcoming **adversity** is actually one of your biggest advantages.

—**commencement address at City College of New York, June 3, 2016**

ADVERSITY (noun): a difficult or challenging situation

PEOPLE CAN ONLY define you if you let them. In the end, it's up to each of us to define ourselves. It's up to us to invent our own future with the choices we make and the actions we take.

—**commencement address at Virginia Tech, May 14, 2012**

AND THOUGH [MY great-grandfathers] didn't live to see it themselves, I can see the smiles on their faces knowing that their great-granddaughters ended up playing ball in the halls of the White House—a magnificent structure built by enslaved Americans.

—**Instagram, June 19, 2020**

OUR GREATNESS HAS never, ever come from sitting back and feeling entitled to what we have.... Our greatness has always come from people who expect nothing and take nothing for granted, folks who work hard for what they have then reach back and help others after them.

—**commencement address at City College of New York,
June 3, 2016**

I LOVE HOW creative and confident Gen Z is, especially the young women. They're far more outspoken and driven than girls were when I was growing up—they don't as quickly **cede** ground to the boys or accept different treatment, and that's terrific. Technology has allowed their entire generation to learn and experience so much so quickly.

—*The National*, **Amtrak, August/September 2019**

> **CEDE** (verb): to give up

WE HAVE TO feel that optimism. For the kids. . . . Progress isn't made through fear. We're experiencing that right now. Fear is the coward's way of leadership. But kids are born into this world with a sense of hope and optimism.

—*O, The Oprah Magazine*, **December 2018**

IF WE WANT to give all of our children a foundation for their dreams, and opportunities worthy of their promise, if we want to give them that sense of limitless possibility, that belief that here in America, there is always something better out there if you're willing to work for it, then we must work like never before.

—Democratic National Convention, September 4, 2012

WE'VE SEEN RECENTLY that the young and diverse America . . . is still here, still hopeful, and still blowing us all away.

—Instagram, July 7, 2020

EDITORIAL NOTE: During the protests of summer 2020, many of the protestors were of the Gen Z and Millennial generations, which are both more racially and ethnically diverse than previous generations in the U.S.

THAT'S BEEN THE most powerful part of the last year—talking with all sorts of young people about how the things that we think are our **inadequacies** are usually our strengths. The simple act of sharing our fears and vulnerabilities helps us embrace our own stories and recognize how much we share with one another.

—*People*, **December 4, 2019**

INADEQUACIES (noun): qualities that are lacking or not good enough

PICK YOURSELF UP, dust yourself off, and keep moving through the pain. Keep. Moving. Forward.

—**commencement address at City College of New York, June 3, 2016**

MY STORY CAN be your story. The details might be a little different, but let me tell you, so many of the challenges and the triumphs will be just the same.

—**Bell Multicultural High School, November 12, 2013**

MILESTONES

1964

- Michelle LaVaughn Robinson is born on January 17
  in Chicago, Illinois to Marian Robinson and Fraser
  Robinson III. Marian works as a secretary at Spiegel, a
  catalog company that markets women's apparel, but later
  stays home to care for Michelle and her older brother,
  Craig. Fraser is a city-pump operator who is pressed into
  becoming a Democratic precinct captain to advance in
  his career. He has multiple sclerosis, which makes his
  mobility increasingly difficult—he walks with a cane
  when Michelle is young, which progresses to a crutch by
  the time Michelle finishes elementary school.

- Michelle grows up on the South Side of Chicago in a
  small apartment on the top floor of a small house on the
  South Shore. She sleeps in a shared bedroom with Craig,
  who is close enough in age—only 21 months older—that
  the children are often mistaken for twins.

- The Robinsons are a close and loving family who speak
  openly with the children about adult topics. Music is a
  central part of family life, and Michelle enjoys listening
  to her father's enormous jazz collection. Family meals
  are usually homemade, and her grandmother makes
  sure there are at least two vegetables on each plate.
  Dinnertime conversations are marked by lively debates
  and plenty of humor. Michelle credits her upbringing

for teaching her the value of caring for the community, working hard, sharing stories, and getting an education.

- The Robinsons teach Michelle and her brother to read by the age of four, and they both skip the second grade. Michelle goes on to study in a gifted program for sixth grade, where she is able to take French and advanced biology classes.

1981

- Michelle graduates as class salutatorian (typically the second-highest ranked student) from Whitney M. Young Magnet High School for gifted children in Chicago. Named for a civil rights leader, it is the first public magnet school in the city, established in 1975 as part of the city's effort to comply with the Supreme Court decision desegregating public schools. The school is an hour away from the Robinson home by city bus, a route that Michelle takes twice a day to get to and from school.

- Michelle, who feels the weight of her parents' and grandparents' sacrifices to invest in her education, takes school seriously and strives for high grades and awards. During her time attending high school, she becomes a member of the National Honor Society, serves as the student council treasurer, and is accepted to her first-choice school, Princeton University, where Craig is already enrolled.

- A first-generation college student (both her parents had enrolled in community college, but did not complete their degrees), Michelle is put into an early orientation program at Princeton to help low-income and minority students prepare for college life. Ultimately, however, it is a difficult adjustment at the school, where the student body is mostly wealthy, white, and male.

- In Michelle's freshman year, she is assigned two roommates, both of whom are white. One of her roommates soon transfers to a single room, but Michelle does not learn until later that this is because the student's mother was upset that her daughter had been assigned a Black roommate.

1985

- Michelle graduates cum laude (with academic distinction) from Princeton University with a B.A. in Sociology and a minor in African American studies. In her thesis, "Princeton-Educated Blacks and the Black Community," she writes that her time at the school has made her more aware of her race than ever before.

- While at Princeton, she is a member of the Organization of Black Unity and an assistant at the Third World Center, which Michelle calls "poorly named but well-intentioned," providing a warm and welcoming place for minority students to connect and receive support. She also creates an after-school reading program for children.

- Michelle enrolls in Harvard Law School.

1988

- Michelle is awarded her J.D. from Harvard Law School. During her time at Harvard, she participates in demonstrations to promote diversity on campus and increase the enrollment of minority students. Throughout her time at law school, she works at Harvard's Legal Aid

Bureau, providing legal assistance to those unable to afford attorneys, and she joins the Black Law Students Association to bring speakers to campus to bring awareness to legal issues and offer career guidance to students.

- After graduation, she begins working as an associate attorney specializing in intellectual property and marketing at Sidley Austin in Chicago.

1989

- Michelle is assigned to mentor Barack Obama, a summer associate and one of the only other Black attorneys at the firm. The firm pairs them in part because Barack is a first-year student at Harvard Law, Michelle's alma mater. Michelle is wary of him before he arrives, tired of her colleagues' excitement over the new intern, and when he shows up late to the first meeting, she is annoyed. But she begins to like him as they get acquainted. Barack asks Michelle out many times but she declines, concerned that a relationship with him would be—as she later says—"tacky," or might complicate their work together. After Barack offers to quit his job so she'll go out with him, she agrees to a date.

- On their first date, the couple sees Spike Lee's *Do the Right Thing*. Outside of a Baskin-Robbins ice cream shop, they share a first kiss. Michelle describes this as the moment she knew the relationship would become a serious one.

1991

- Michelle's father, Fraser Robinson III, dies at the age of 55.

- Following the death of her father, Michelle reevaluates her career in corporate law. Wanting to honor the values of her parents and follow the work she finds most rewarding, she dedicates herself to serving communities and neighborhoods. She continues to pursue public service throughout her career.

- Bolstered by her love of her hometown, Michelle takes a position as assistant to Chicago mayor Richard M. Daley. There, she works with Valerie Jarrett, whom she introduces to Barack. Jarrett would go on to become one of Barack's senior advisors and a high-profile part of his presidential administration.

- After her time in the mayor's office, Michelle becomes assistant commissioner of planning and development in Chicago's City Hall.

- Michelle and Barack become engaged.

1992

- On October 3, Michelle and Barack are married at the Trinity United Church of Christ in Chicago. They recite their own vows and dance their first dance as a married couple to Stevie Wonder's "You and I." The couple honeymoons on the California coast.

- The newlyweds move into an apartment in Chicago's Hyde Park neighborhood.

1993

- Michelle becomes the Founding Executive Director of the new Chicago chapter of Public Allies, an AmeriCorps program established during Bill Clinton's administration. This youth leadership training program equips young adults with skills needed for careers in public service, a mission that is close to Michelle's heart. While at Public Allies, she goes door-to-door recruiting youth for the program and sets impressive fundraising records that stand for over a decade after her departure.

1996

- Michelle leaves her position at Public Allies to become the Associate Dean of Student Services at the University of Chicago. She is also Director of the University Community Service Center, where she works to further develop the school's first student-run community service organization. In her new role, Michelle provides students with service opportunities throughout the city of Chicago. During her time working at the University of Chicago, the volunteerism rate on campus soars.

- Although she is initially against Barack entering politics due to her distaste for politicians and the instability of political life, she actively supports his campaign for Illinois State Senate, which he wins, by going door to door for signatures and fundraising.

1998

- On July 4, Michelle gives birth to the Obamas' first daughter, Malia. Though she doesn't reveal it publicly until the publication of her memoir in 2018, the couple had struggled with infertility, and Michelle had had a miscarriage before Malia's birth, after which they sought medical help in the form of IVF treatments to conceive.

1999

- While campaigning for the Democratic primary for Illinois's First Congressional District, Barack stays with Malia, who is very ill, and misses a vote on a major bill. The backlash he receives from opponents for staying home to care for his sick infant fuels Michelle's frustration with politics.

2000

- Michelle supports Barack throughout an unsuccessful primary challenge to United States Representative Bobby Rush, which Barack later calls "an ill-considered race." He loses to his opponent, a former Black Panther leader with great local popularity, by more than 30 points.

2001

- On June 10, the Obamas' second daughter, Natasha (known as Sasha), is born.

2002

- After taking four-month-old Sasha to an interview at the University of Chicago Hospitals, Michelle is offered a position as Executive Director of Community and External Affairs. As her career accelerates and Barack tends to legislative business away from home, Malia and Sasha remain Michelle's biggest priority, and she seeks out ways to maintain a good work-life balance. She goes on to speak about the importance of support and flexibility in the workplace for working families throughout her career.

2004

- Barack is elected to the United States Senate, taking office in 2005. Michelle is active in his campaign, and the election, along with Barack's popular speech at the 2004 Democratic National Convention, brings national attention to the family.

- At the Democratic National Convention, minutes before Barack walks on stage to deliver what would become a breakout speech, Michelle offers her husband words of encouragement: "Just don't screw it up, buddy." When asked for comment about her husband's performance at the Convention, she responds with understatement: "Must've been a good speech."

2005

- Michelle is promoted to Vice President of Community Relations and External Affairs at the University of Chicago Medical Center, where she works to improve access to medical care and encourages the hospital to adopt new practices to support all patients, such as hiring people who work on behalf a patient's health and well-being.

- With the intention of bringing the hospital's services to the communities of Chicago, Michelle begins serving

on the boards of the University of Chicago Laboratory
Schools and the Chicago Council on Global Affairs.

- While seeking to gain experience in corporate manage-
  ment, Michelle is elected director on the board of Tree-
  House Foods, Inc., a food manufacturer and distributor,
  where she serves on the audit and corporate governance
  committees.

2006

- When Barack's candidacy for president is first discussed,
  Michelle joins the strategy meetings. She has concerns
  about how the campaign will raise enough money
  to compete with Hillary Clinton and other primary
  candidates and demands a concrete plan from Barack's
  advisors.

2007

- Michelle resigns from her position on the board of Tree-
  House Foods, Inc. She cites the inability to effectively
  split her time between her family, the campaign, and her
  professional responsibilities, although some speculate
  that the company's ties to Walmart clashed with her
  husband's opposition to their labor practices.

- Michelle reduces her hours at the University of Chicago
  Medical Center to become more involved in Barack's
  campaign leading up to the state primaries, speaking to
  groups across the country.

- In October, she participates in the first forum of political
  spouses ever held, gathering nearly every spouse of

Democratic and Republican presidential candidates at
the Women's Conference in California.

2008

- Michelle plays a major role in Barack's 2008 presidential campaign. In her speaking engagements, Michelle
  connects with her audiences by sharing her own stories
  and life experiences, drawing connections between those
  experiences and her husband's campaign goals. She gains
  a reputation as being more direct than her husband,
  which allows her to address more divisive topics and
  voice frustrations that Barack is less willing to discuss.
  This cements her place in the public eye and opens her to
  increasing criticism from voters, the media, and political
  opponents.

- While campaigning, Michelle leaves Malia and Sasha
  with her mother, Marian. She sometimes delays
  speeches so she can talk to them on the phone, a fact
  that she shares with her audiences. "Thank God for
  Grandma!" is a refrain on the campaign trail.

- At a campaign stop in February ahead of the Wisconsin
  primary, Michelle thanks supporters for the overwhelm-
  ing support they have given Barack and his plans for
  change in Washington. On the spur of the moment, she
  tells the audience, "For the first time in my adult life, I
  am really proud of my country because it feels like hope
  is finally making a comeback." These words are quickly
  used against her and her husband's candidacy, as critics
  suggest the couple is radical and un-American. Though
  she clarifies and walks back the statement, it is a difficult
  moment that follows Michelle throughout the campaign.

- Michelle delivers a speech at the Democratic National Convention that is praised by media outlets and wins admiration from the public that reflects in the polls. Skilled at gaining the support of undecided voters at campaign stops, she earns the nickname "the closer" within the campaign.

- Although she continues in her role at University of Chicago Hospitals during the primary campaign, Michelle switches to part-time work, both to accommodate her work on her husband's campaign and to allow her to spend more time with her daughters. She eventually takes a leave of absence.

- During an interview on *The Tonight Show* hosted by Jay Leno, Michelle appears in a gold skirt and matching cardigan over a silk blouse. When asked about where she bought the outfit—which had been chosen in response to a recent revelation that Sarah Palin, then the Republican vice-presidential candidate, had a campaign clothing budget of $150,000—Michelle proudly responds, "J. Crew." The moment vaulted the retailer to newfound popularity and resonated with women across the country, who admired both Michelle's style and down to earth selection. Throughout her time as First Lady, Michelle's fashion choices—often bold and revealing of her personality—are followed with a fervor likened to that devoted to Jacqueline Kennedy.

- Barack wins the presidential election and in his victory speech, he thanks Michelle for the sacrifices she has made, the resilience of her support in his campaign, and for being "the rock" that grounded their family.

2009

- On January 20, Michelle becomes the First Lady of the United States, also becoming the first Black First Lady in American history. She identifies three main objectives on which to focus during her time as First Lady: help working parents find a healthy work-life balance, provide support to American military families, and encourage a rise in community service.

- Michelle begins her outreach as her husband begins his presidency, visiting homeless shelters, soup kitchens, and schools. Her favorability ratings are about 75 percent, up from 43 percent during the campaign, rising especially among groups that had previously criticized her.

- Michelle's highest priority in the White House is taking care of her daughters while living under the intense examination of the public. In their early life at the White House, the Ty Inc. toy company introduces new dolls named "Sweet Sasha" and "Marvelous Malia." Michelle is displeased with the company using her daughters' names for marketing, and Ty Inc. quickly discontinues the dolls.

- In March, Michelle facilitates the creation of the White House's first vegetable garden since Eleanor Roosevelt's Victory Garden. She is inspired not only by Roosevelt but also by the stories of her grandmother tending a victory garden in Chicago when Michelle's mother was a child. The White House Garden, which consists of various vegetables and herbs, is planted and harvested by elementary students in the area to educate them on food and to enjoy the benefits of their labor. She also has beehives installed to encourage pollination.

- Michelle serves on the board of directors of the Chicago Council on Global Affairs.

- ABC's Barbara Walters names Michelle her "most fascinating person" of the year. In the accompanying interview, Michelle describes the most difficult part of her job as First Lady as the "constant concern" that she is doing enough to make the country proud. She also states that although Barack would have given up his political career if she had asked him, she thinks that she made the right decision in supporting him.

- Although she often positions herself as a mother and wife first, Michelle is engaged in politics. She hosts a White House reception for women's rights activists to mark the enactment of the Lilly Ledbetter Fair Pay Act of 2009, which amends the Voting Rights Act of 1964 in expanding the timeframe in which someone can file a lawsuit against pay discrimination by an employer. She also supports the economic stimulus bill during the Great Recession, which focuses on job creation and economic assistance, and makes plans to visit all Cabinet-level agencies as she accustoms herself to Washington.

2010

- Michelle campaigns for Democrats in the midterm elections.

- After a surprising discussion with her pediatrician, who raises concerns about her daughters' weight gain, Michelle decides to focus on health and nutrition—not just for her kids, but for kids nationwide. She launches her Let's Move! campaign to address childhood obesity by helping schools provide healthier meals, encouraging kids to be more active, and supporting parents' efforts to make healthier choices for their children.

- *Forbes* names Michelle Obama the most powerful woman in the world.

- Michelle appears in *The Hooping Life*, a documentary to promote hula-hooping for health.

- Barack signs the Healthy, Hunger-Free Kids Act, a bill which reauthorizes many child nutrition programs through 2015, including the National School Lunch and Breakfast programs and the Special Supplemental Nutrition Program for Women, Infants and Children (WIC). Michelle praises the passage of the bill as foundational to the work of her Let's Move! initiative.

2011

- Michelle launches the Joining Forces initiative along with Dr. Jill Biden. This initiative is intended to support veterans, service members, and their families by educating the public about their experiences, creating a connection between the general public and military families, and developing wellness, education, and employment opportunities for service members and their families. It is largely successful, especially in the area of increasing employment for both veterans and military spouses.

2012

- Barack wins reelection and remains President for a second term. Michelle is more involved in his campaign than she was in 2008. Although still seen as a polarizing figure, she is considered more popular than her husband, with an open and approachable persona.

- In May, Michelle and Barack announce their support of same-sex marriage. This is Michelle's first time commenting on the issue.

- Michelle publishes *American Grown: The Story of the White House Kitchen Garden and Gardens Across America*, which documents her experience with the White House Garden throughout the season and the connection between health and quality food.

- At the site of Michelle and Barack's first kiss outside the Baskin-Robbins in Hyde Park, a plaque is installed on a 3,000-pound boulder to memorialize their love.

2014

- Michelle launches the Reach Higher initiative to help students pursue their education beyond high school, with a special focus on low-income and first-generation college students. The initiative highlights college access and financial aid resources, exposes students to career and summer learning opportunities, and supports school counselors who work directly with students.

- Michelle works together with the FDA to make changes to nutrition labels on food. The new changes include making calorie counts bigger and bolder, listing added sugars, and making serving sizes more proportionate.

- Michelle makes a guest appearance on *Parks and Recreation*, playing herself.

2015

- Michelle and Barack launch Let Girls Learn, an initiative dedicated to helping improve adolescent girls' access to education worldwide through a broad variety of programs and partnerships. During press events announcing the initiative, Michelle shares stories of young girls from around the world who have overcome poverty, violence, and other obstacles to attain an education, citing them as inspiration for the work.

- Michelle, along with her daughters and mother, stay at Kensington Palace and have tea with Prince Harry. Michelle and the Prince discuss helping military families as well as the Let Girls Learn initiative.

- Welcoming thousands of athletes, Michelle kicks off the Special Olympics World Games in Los Angeles.

- After the landmark Supreme Court decision *Obergefell v. Hodges*, which legalized same-sex marriage throughout the United States, the administration honors the decision with a rainbow light display projected on the White House. In her 2018 memoir, Michelle reveals that that night, she and Malia, then 16 years old, snuck out of the residence past Secret Service agents to witness the public's emotional celebration.

2016

- Along with endorsing Hillary Clinton as the Democratic presidential nominee, Michelle makes several campaign speeches both with and for her. Her efforts are unprec-edented—no sitting First Lady has ever campaigned so prominently for a former political rival, much less a former First Lady.

- Michelle holds her last garden-planting event at the White House, a tradition established to help educate kids on the importance of healthy foods. She ends the event by saying she hopes the subsequent administrations uphold the tradition of feeding and educating children through the garden.

- Michelle Obama appears in a one-on-one interview with Oprah Winfrey on a special, "First Lady Michelle Obama Says Farewell to the White House," in which she reveals her belief that her husband's administration achieved its goal of giving hope to the American people.

2017

- Michelle and Barack move out of the White House and retire their titles of President and First Lady.

- In her parting remarks as First Lady, Michelle says serv-ing the country was the greatest honor of her life.

2018

- Michelle publishes her memoir *Becoming* on November 13, which details her life's journey from Chicago to the White House. It quickly becomes a #1 *New York Times* Best Seller.

- She is voted the woman most admired by Americans according to Gallup's annual survey, removing Hillary Clinton from the spot for the first time in 17 years.

- Marian Robinson, when asked in an interview what about her daughter made her proudest, says, "When I grow up, I would like to be like Michelle Obama."

2019

- Gallup names Michelle the most admired woman in the world for the second year in a row.

- The *Michelle Obama: Forward Motion* documentary is created to showcase Michelle's life journey from Chicago's South Side to the White House.

- In response to racist tweets from Donald Trump against Alexandria Ocasio-Cortez, Ayanna Pressley, Ilhan Omar, and Rashida Tlaib—the four congresswomen of color often referred to as "the Squad"—Michelle tweets, "What really makes this country great is its diversity."

2020

- Netflix releases *Becoming*, a documentary about Michelle's tour for her book of the same name.

- Michelle begins a PBS KIDS Read-Along Series on TV called "Mondays with Michelle Obama," where she reads her favorite children's books to kids.

- In July, Michelle launches *The Michelle Obama Podcast*, with Barack as her first guest.

- The *Becoming* audiobook wins Michelle a Grammy for Best Spoken Word Album.

- Michelle and Barack serve as executive producers on *Crip Camp: A Disability Revolution*, a documentary about a summer camp for teens with disabilities, many of whom went on to become activists in the disability rights movement of the 1970s.

- Michelle and Barack reveal they are working on producing a Netflix series called *Listen to Your Vegetables & Eat Your Parents* to teach young children and parents about the origins of health food around the globe.

- It is announced that Viola Davis will star as Michelle Obama in the upcoming Showtime drama series *First Ladies*.

2021

- During the U.S. Senate runoff election in Georgia, Michelle encourages Georgia voters to go to the polls, supporting Democratic candidates Raphael Warnock and Jon Ossoff. Both candidates win in a state that has not had a Democratic U.S. senator since 2005.

- On January 20, 2021, Michelle and Barack attend the inauguration of President Joe Biden, Barack's former vice president.

- Michelle is inducted into the National Women's Hall of Fame, a museum and nonprofit organization that honors the achievements of American women throughout history.

GLOSSARY

ADVERSITY	(noun): a difficult or challenging situation
ANTIDOTE	(noun): a remedy that soothes or reduces harm
ASPIRE	(verb): to want to reach a certain life goal or achievement
BASTION	(noun): a protected place
BOISTEROUS	(adj.): noisy and full of energy
BONDAGE	(noun): enslavement
BURGEONING	(adj.): growing or developing
CAVALIER	(adj.): acting in a dismissive or uncaring manner
CEDE	(verb): to give up
CHANNELED	(verb): directed energy in a specific way
COMPORTED	(verb): behaved in a way that is considered appropriate to a certain situation or role
CORRODE	(verb): slowly destroy
DEVASTATING	(adj.): causing significant emotional or physical harm
DIRE	(adj.): very serious in nature
DISPIRITING	(adj.): prompting a lack of hope or excitement
DIVISIVE	(adj.): prompting disagreement and often leading to the formation of opposing points of view or groups
EMINENTLY	(adv.): highly
EMPATHY	(noun): the ability to understand and be sensitive to the feelings or thoughts of another person

EMPOWERED	(adj.): feeling confident and supported
EXACERBATED	(verb): made more extreme
EXHILARATING	(adj.): causing strong feelings of happiness and excitement
GRAVITATE	(verb): to be drawn to a person, place, or idea
HARBOR	(verb): to hold on to certain feelings for a long period of time
HIERARCHY	(noun): a classification system where people are placed into a ranking order, with one group at the top and one at the bottom
INADEQUACIES	(noun): qualities that are lacking or not good enough
INEVITABLE	(adj.): unavoidable
INITIATIVE	(noun): a plan or policy that is designed to solve a particular issue
INOCULATE	(verb): protect against harm
INSPIRATIONS	(noun): people, places, or experiences that move one to act, create, or pursue something
INTEGRITY	(noun): the quality of having strong moral values
LUXURIATING	(verb): indulging in an activity or experience that is enjoyable
MAGNITUDE	(noun): large in importance and size
MANDATE	(noun): order or command
MANDATORY	(adj.): required
NOURISH	(verb): feed in a sustainable and satisfying way
NUTRITIOUS	(adj.): possessing the types of vitamins and other elements that people need to stay healthy

PERSUASIONS	(noun): closely held opinions, values, or beliefs
PHILOSOPHY	(noun): an idea about how people should live or behave
POTENT	(adj.): very strong or effective
RATIONALIZE	(verb): explain with reason or logic
RESILIENCE	(noun): the ability to find happiness or success after facing challenges or hardships
RITUALS	(noun): actions that are repeated multiple times in the same way
SALVE	(noun): a remedy that is soothing
SAVOR	(verb): fully enjoy or appreciate
SOCIO-ECONOMIC BACKGROUND	(noun): related to social and economic factors, such as a person or family's financial situation, education, and access to resources
SOCIOECONOMIC CLASS	(noun): standing in a society related to social and economic factors, such as a person or family's financial situation, education, and access to resources
SUPERFICIAL	(adj.): on a surface level
TEMPERED	(verb): lessened or made less powerful
TRANSCENDS	(verb): overcomes limits or boundaries
UNFLINCHING	(adj.): refusing to turn away from an unpleasant situation
VULNERABILITY	(noun): a quality of emotional openness that often reveals a person's fears or weaknesses

ADDITIONAL RESOURCES

Dillon, Molly. *Yes She Can: 10 Stories of Hope & Change from Young Female Staffers of the Obama White House*. Schwartz & Wade, 2019.
- A collection of essays written by young women who were part of the Obama administration.

Evans, Marta and Hannah Masters (editors). *Michelle Obama: In Her Own Words*. Agate Publishing, 2021.
- This is the full-length title from which this Young Adult Readers edition was created. The full-length version includes additional quotations from Michelle Obama.

Hallgren, Nadia. *Becoming*. Netflix, 2020.
- A documentary film focused on Michelle Obama's life during the book tour for her memoir, *Becoming*.

Hill, Jordan. *Michelle Obama: Forward Motion*. E M Productions. 2019.
- This hour-long documentary film tells Michelle Obama's life story.

Lucidon, Amanda. *Chasing Light: Michelle Obama Through the Lens of a White House Photographer*. Ten Speed Press, 2017.
- This book was written by a White House photographer who spent four years working with Michelle Obama.

Moore, Natalie. *The South Side: A Portrait of Chicago and American Segregation*. Picador Paper, 2019.
- This book discusses Chicago's history, with a particular

focus on the South Side and the history and politics of racial segregation in Chicago.

Obama, Michelle. *Becoming*. Crown, 2018.
* This is Michelle Obama's memoir. There is also a Young Readers version of this book, published in 2021.

Obama, Michelle. *American Grown: The Story of the White House Kitchen Garden and Gardens Across America*. Crown, 2012.
* Michelle Obama describes her work on the White House Garden and lessons that can be applied to gardens in other places.

Obama, Michelle. *The Michelle Obama Podcast*. Spotify. June 2020 – April 2021.
* Each episode of this podcast features Michelle Obama talking with people in her life, including family, friends, colleagues, and celebrities, about a variety of topics.

obamawhitehouse.archives.gov/administration/first-lady-michelle-obama
* The Obama White House has been archived online, and Michelle has her own page. This site includes links to initiatives she led as First Lady, such as *Let's Move!* and *Let Girls Learn*.

cnn.com/2016/07/26/politics/transcript-michelle-obama-speech-democratic-national-convention/index.html
* A video and transcript of Michelle Obama's now famous speech delivered in support of Hillary Clinton at the 2016 Democratic National Convention.

Acknowledgments

We would like to thank Kelsey Dame, Emily Feng, Paige Gilberg, Rachel Hinton, Marilyn Isaacks, Eva López, Claire Maclauchlan, Elizabeth Pappas, Briana Rooke, Erin Rosenberg, Annie Schmitt, Suzanne Sonnier, and Sherry Welch for their invaluable contributions to the preparation of this manuscript.